Dedication:

To our Mum, who is always there for us.

Mrs Nitsa Michael

Published by Rotherfield Studio Ltd

Printed by Berforts Limited, Hastings, UK

ISBN 978-0-95665-601-8

Grand Pier Limited
Marine Parade, Weston-super-Mare, Somerset BS23 1AL
Registered In England & Wales: No. 152507

www.grandpier.co.uk

Introduction

Growing up at Knightstone on Weston-super-Mare seafront, I would get out of bed every morning, open the curtains and there it was – the Grand Pier. It dominated the entire landscape. As a kid, I wanted to go to the Pier every day. I wasn't allowed, but it never stopped me wanting to go.

It was a complete surprise when the Pier was offered to us. We had never considered owning it and I didn't think the previous owners would sell it, as it had been in the same family for three generations. We immediately dismissed the opportunity.

For the next two weeks, on my way to and from work, I would find myself driving along the sea front and just staring at the Grand Pier. The more I looked at it, the more I knew we had to buy it – after all, who gets the opportunity to buy their very own Pier? I knew it was an opportunity that we couldn't turn down.

The fire was utterly devastating. It felt like someone else's nightmare and we were just looking in from outside, but it was a very real situation and we had to face up to it.

There was never any doubt in my mind that we would re-build the Pavilion. Within hours of the fire we held a press conference and I announced we would re-build it. The fire had happened on our watch and we felt obligated to the whole town, we just had to re-build it. The task took over our lives for the next two years.

First came the demolition works, followed by the repair and renovation of the sub-structure steelwork. Once this was complete, seventy new steel piles, some more than thirty metres in length, were driven into the bedrock to carry the new building and rides.

The Princess Royal gave everyone a big lift when she visited the Pier in October 2008. It was fantastic to host HRH on the Pier and she was very interested to hear about the fire and how we were going about rebuilding this iconic structure.

The Pavilion building is just a quarter of a mile out to sea, but it may as well be twenty miles out. The weight limit on the original section just added to the difficulties and logistics of building something that big out at sea. The problems we encountered have surprised us all.

I would like to thank everyone involved in the reconstruction of this fantastic building. Weston-super-Mare Grand Pier is fully restored to its former glory and we are extremely proud of it.

Kerry Michael

Pier Owner

1933-2008

The iconic structure lit up in its trademark green.

It was enchanting inside and out, welcoming 25,000 visitors on a busy day.

The Fire:
28th July 2008

Black smoke engulfs the Pavilion, choking the fun of the fair.

It is believed the seat of the fire was located in the north-east tower.

Once the fire took hold it took less than 90 minutes for the Pavilion to be completely destroyed.

At the height of the inferno, temperatures reached 1200 degrees.

Due to thick black smoke filling the skyline above Weston-super-Mare the fire could be seen up to 60 miles away.

80 Firemen attended to the blaze.

The life and soul of the Pier was completely destroyed by the fire.

After the Fire

An estimated 700 tonnes of twisted steel was all that remained of the Pavilion.

Amongst the lost beams were a number of vehicles.

An eerie silence fell about the Pier.

The damage was surveyed as soon as possible and an exclusion zone was created.
Public safety was paramount.

A safe lies lodged in the twisted metalwork.

Money was packed tightly in the safe which stopped it from burning.

Not all coins could be saved; this cash box was originally part of a fruit machine.

The clean up operation took several weeks. Melted coins from the arcade machines were put into a cement mixer to break them up before being hand sorted. The Royal Mint would only accept coins that were clearly recognisable.

Three days after the fire the shore end reopened. Visitors were able to view the destroyed Pavilion and gathered in disbelief.

Visitors had the opportunity to write in a book of condolence. Many left donations, which were used to part fund a scale model of the Pier.

On 5th September 2008 crowds gathered at the Pier's entrance to await the arrival of the Princess Royal.

The Princess Royal gave everyone a huge lift when she visited the Pier.

Despite the devastation, on 27th August 2008 the Grand Pier played host to the Red Arrows.

The Red Arrows put on a spectacular display which was viewed by thousands.

The Plans

The Winning design by Angus Meek.

Ray Hole Architects.

Stride Treglown.

Acanthus Furguson Mann.

Grimshaw.

AWW.

Kerry Michael submitting the planning application to North Somerset Council on December 7th 2008. Planning permission was granted on March 12th 2009.

Reconstructing
an Icon

700 Tonnes of steel were removed during the demolition.

The skeletal remains of the Freefall ride.

The deck cleared of debris ready for reconstruction to start.

The site was handed over to contractors John Sisk and Son who would start the rebuild of this 21st Century Icon.

Extra large feet were made for the Jack-up barge to stop it sinking into the sand.

70 new piles were driven into the seabed to support the building.

All of these piles, acting together are capable of supporting a weight of 10 million kilograms.

The ground under the Pier is so soft that most of the piles sank more than 10 metres under their own weight. They were then driven down into the bedrock.

The piling process took an average of four hours per pile!

Two vehicles involved in the reconstruction become victims of the second highest rising tide in the World.

The first steels rise above the deck.

25 Roofers erected 5000 square metres of roofing and builders put up 3600 square metres of cladding.

The Grand Pier was the biggest scaffolding job in Europe during the construction process.

A scaffold ramp was erected to enable the roof sheets to be manufactured and installed in single long lengths up to 90 metres each.

Fibreglass roofs to the four turrets.

The internal volume of the Pier would hold 570 London buses or 400 million sticks of rock.

A topping out ceremony celebrated the completion of the roof.

In early June, there were more than 400 construction workers on site.

The British Association of Leisure Parks, Piers and Attractions visited the Pier on 15th October 2009.

Although still an active building site The Grand Pier hosted the Sport Relief Mile
in March 2010.

Raised access floors afford maximum flexibility in the new building.

20,000 new decking planks were used around the Pier.

A covered walkway was installed to allow people to travel the quarter of a mile to the Pavilion in the dry.

Construction of the 50 seater 4D cinema complete with 12 special effects.

Escalators are installed to make travel between floors quick and simple.

The new drop tower is 5 metres taller than the previous one!

F1simulator - a full size replica complete with force-feedback controls and surround sound. Used by Formula 1 racing teams.

The House of Horrors, a new version of an old favourite.

20 Karts, electric floor. The biggest ride on the Pier.

The double helix Helter Skelter occupies the North West tower and is 14.5 metres high.

The Laser Maze, a real 21st century ride.

The biggest thrill on a pier - Robocoaster will leave everyone in a spin.

The 8 seater Sidewinder being installed and tested.

Grand Pier Recruitment Day - March 2010

Weston's finest talent applying to work on The Grand Pier.

Entertainment was provided throughout the day.

Thousands of people queued from 4am to be the first on the Grand Pier when it opened at 10am on 23rd October 2010.

Visitors rushed up the waist to be the first to see the new Pavilion.

Queues formed quickly inside the Great Hall on opening day.

Visitors enjoy the rides.

All the fun of the fair is restored.